Published by Creative Education
P.O. Box 227, Mankato, Minnesota 56002
Creative Education is an imprint of
The Creative Company
www.thecreativecompany.us

Design and production by The Design Lab
Art direction by Rita Marshall
Printed by Corporate Graphics in the
United States of America

Photographs by Alamy (Arco Images GmbH, Bryan
& Cherry Alexander Photography, Deco, Stone
Nature Photography), Corbis (Daniel J. Cox, Layne
Kennedy, W. Perry Conway), Dreamstime (Dmitrij),
and iStockphoto (Steve Geer, Nathan Hobbs,
Jim Kruger)

Library of Congress Cataloging-in-Publication Data
Riggs, Kate.
Wolves / by Kate Riggs.
p. cm. — (Amazing animals)
Includes index.
Summary: A basic exploration of the appearance,
behavior, and habitat of wolves, a family of wild
dogs. Also included is a story from folklore explain-
ing why wolves are different from domestic dogs.
ISBN 978-1-58341-991-5
1. Wolves—Juvenile literature. I. Title. II. Series.
QL737.C22R536 2011
599.773—dc22   2009047735

CPSIA: 040110 PO1128

5816

First Edition
9 8 7 6 5 4 3 2 1

WOLVES

BY KATE RIGGS

CREATIVE EDUCATION

Wolves are big, wild dogs.

Most wolves are called gray wolves. One other kind of wolf is called a red wolf. There are 17 kinds of gray wolves in the world.

Gray wolves have thick fur. Their coats can be gray, white, black, or brown. They have bushy tails, too. Red wolves have shorter fur. They look like big foxes.

A red wolf has big ears that help it to hear well

Male gray wolves are the biggest wolves. They weigh from 90 to 175 pounds (41–79 kg). Males are five feet (1.5 m) long. Females are a little smaller. Red wolves can weigh about 60 pounds (27 kg).

Gray wolves are bigger than most kinds of pet dogs

*Gray wolves do not mind
cold and snowy winters*

Most gray wolves live in northern parts of the world. These places get very cold in the winter. Some gray wolves live near **mountains**. Red wolves live only in the southeastern part of the United States.

mountains very big hills made of rock

Wolves eat meat. Some of their favorite animals to eat are moose, deer, and bighorn sheep. Sometimes wolves eat smaller animals like rabbits and fish, too.

A gray wolf may eat 20 pounds (9 kg) of meat at once

Wolf pups hide in a den
when their mother is gone

A mother wolf has four to seven **pups** at a time. At first, the pups stay in a **den** with their mother. When the pups are about two months old, they leave the den. They start learning how to hunt. Wild wolves can live 10 to 12 years.

pups baby wolves

den a home that is hidden, like a cave

Wolves live in groups called packs. Most packs have about six to nine wolves. Two wolves called the alpha (*AL-fuh*) male and the alpha female lead the pack. Wolves do a lot of napping, playing, and moving around.

Wolves can see well in the dark and like to hunt at night

*Gray wolves have big feet
and can run fast over snow*

Wolves spend a lot of time looking for food. They hunt for up to 10 hours a day. The pack works together to chase prey. Wolves have to run fast to catch a deer or a moose!

prey animals that are eaten by other animals

Today, some people go to see wolves in the wild. Other people visit zoos to see wolves. It is exciting to see these beautiful animals run and howl!

Wolves howl to "talk" to other wolves in the pack

A Wolf Story

How are wolves and dogs different? A Greek man named Aesop (*EE-sop*) used to tell a story about this. One day, a wolf and a dog met on a road. The dog told the wolf that he should live with people. Then the wolf would have an easy life because he would not have to hunt for food. But if he lived with people, he would not be free. Wolves always choose to be free animals instead of getting free food.

Read More

Ling, Mary. *Amazing Wolves, Dogs, & Foxes*. New York: Knopf, 1991.

Simon, Seymour. *Wolves*. New York: HarperCollins, 2009.

Web Sites

Enchanted Learning: Red Wolves
http://www.enchantedlearning.com/subjects/mammals/dog/Redwolfprintout.shtml
This site has red wolf facts and a picture to color.

National Geographic Kids Creature Feature: Gray Wolves
http://kids.nationalgeographic.com/Animals/CreatureFeature/Graywolf
This site has pictures and videos of gray wolves.

Index